To Richard & Rhian

– best !

M25 BLUES

NATHAN GOODE

MINERVA PRESS
MONTREUX LONDON WASHINGTON

M25 BLUES

ISBN 1 85863 926 3

First Published 1996 by
MINERVA PRESS
195 Knightsbridge
London SW7 1RE

Printed in Great Britain by
B.W.D. Ltd., Northolt, Middlesex

M25 BLUES

For my father, John Goode.

CONTENTS

M25 BLUES

I'm done with dancing to Mammon's tune,
Tired of scaling monetary peaks
Where a number's as real as the Man in the Moon,
Oh take me back to MacGillycuddy's Reeks.

We've got:

Traffic jams; signal failure; cappuccino at Angelo's; yet another John Grisham novel; photochemical smog; company cars; multi-screen cinemas; Sky, cable and interactive media; row upon row of miserable closed faces on the buses, the tubes and the trains; the M25; flight paths; camcorders; Wimbledon, Henley and Ascot; cones hotlines; corporate hospitality; estate agents; Sainsbury's free-range spicy Mexican style crispy over-packaged beaver chips; Merchant Ivory, Kenneth Branagh and the RSC; Barbours and their imitators; Armani glasses; the Brit Awards; pulp fiction, pulp reality; slippery politicians invading your sitting-room; antique reproduction Swedish Shaker radiator covers; private health insurance, private schools, private lives; designer beers; Jermyn Street quality at affordable prices; sticky scorching summers; wheelclamps; CBI, TQM, MBA; M-registrations; interest-free credit; *Evening Standard* columnists; Gucci; highlights and lowlights; Reebok; Bugs Bunny ties; Michael Bolton and Barry Manilow; Sylvester Stallone opening his heart to *The Sun*; accountants; abusive Heathrow cab-drivers; Oprah Winfrey; Peter Lilley; Bob Monkhouse...

Let's burn these worldly vanities,
Those silly small urbanities
And petty grey mundanities:
You'll find me on the Reeks.

FETISH

When I hear the word 'fornication'
I f-feel this tingle up my spine
Said the woman on the Number Twenty-Three.
The frisson's - dare I say it - sexual.
In this jaded old faded old world we live in
You've got to get your kicks from somewhere.
On Saturdays we challenge the wolves
To Noel Edmonds on videotape
Backwards

Albert wears lace beneath his tank top
My nightie's made from finest clingfilm
We keep the Marmite in the bedroom
Our washing powder's edged with rubber
We've trained the dog to use the camera
Our three-piece suite is filled with water
You've got to get your kicks from somewhere
Said the woman on the Number Twenty-Three.

THE LESSON

When will my people learn?
Said God.
When the seas are empty,
When the rivers are dry,
When the trees are dead,
When the earth is poisoned,
When the cities are choking,
When the people are dying,
When there's nothing to watch
On TV.
By then space travel will be a reality.
Huge ships will fill with people
And set off like the pilgrim fathers
For another green and life-giving planet.
The hell they will,
Said God.
Not if I can help it.

WAVERING

I dunno.
It's tough being a superhero.
Maybe I need a change.
His squire had laid out the armour
Neatly
In two piles,
White to his right,
Gleaming with righteousness.
The sword is clean and true,
Decapitates with barely a whisper.
To his left
The alternative offering,
Blacker than a thousand plagues
Axe, mace, helmet crested high
With predatory raven.
Slay the infidel or massacre the innocents?
The tyrant's sirens and
The clergy's blandishments
Try his ears.
Darkness and light fuse before his eyes
On the battleground.

Arnulf sighed as he picked his way between the inconsequential piles of metal,
His bare feet slapping softly on the stone flags.
He pushed open the door at the end of the hall
And stepped into the mottled sunlight
Of his garden.

WOULD MR SERRISIER PLEASE SEE THE LADY IN THE TICKET OFFICE - THANK YOU

Ah Mr Serrisier
Please come in
Do
Be seated
Can I see proof of identity?
Thank you, that's perfect.
Before I start, Mr Serrisier
I should just like to say
That I admire you through my window
Every day. I admire
Your suits - invariably pinstriped - they seem perfectly tailored
To the contours
(Or should I say lack of them)
Of your ramrod body. Your legs
Straighter than your rolled umbrella
A good woman would die for them
As she would for your ascetic, minimalist torso.
I could be that woman, Mr Serrisier
I sit in this molehole day after day
Thinking of sugar cane, dusty roads and cool blue mountains
Of my childhood in the sun
Perhaps I brought some of that sun with me
To this dreary grey land.
My grandfather died a few weeks ago
I stand to inherit his scruffy colonial house,
A few impoverished acres
And a hundred laughing relatives and friends.
My home is in Balham
But my heart is in Jamaica
Why don't you join me, Mr Serrisier?
We've paid our taxes and our dues
We've tried to live and love amid the rain and the dirt
I could dress you in fruit-patterned shorts
Feed you prawn and pineapple
Give you cocktails of rum and exotic fruits

As you watch the sun set from the creaking verandah.
Throw off the chains of your climate and your Empire
Mr Serrisier
I could teach you to be black and happy.
I beg your pardon?
Why I wanted to see you?
Your season ticket
Was found in the booking hall, Mr Serrisier
Here it is
No, thank *you* Mr Serrisier
Have a nice day.

UNTITLED I

Serendipity, he murmured through his cherry wine,
Playing spinning tops with his parasol,
Pausing only to jab thoughtfully at the green plastic monkey
Clinging to his glass.
Serendipity dresses in cut-off jeans and fraying running shoes.
She jogs through puddles under bridges
And shies from the sun.
She eats lottery tickets and laughs at game show hosts,
Walks under ladders
And dances on cracks in the pavement.
She plays poker with the Grim Reaper
And loses
Tosses her head and slaps his bony shoulder;
Chalks up another deficit on the slate.
Serendipity weaves a web of broken causes
She curries our hope,
Clothes the unthinkable.
I know she likes me,
He muttered to the barman
Whose sour cloth smeared sticky rings from the glasses
Wider across the counter
I could make her mine
If only I could find her.

WINTERSTING

A morning in October
As clear as glass
Premature frost stiffens the grass
Poetry is about having nothing to say
Said the gnome
And a lopsided grin creased
His weather-eaten face
We have a monarchy, which shames us
Whispered the Muscovy cat from the safety of the garden fence.
We get the royalty we deserve, i suppose
And her tail flicked angrily at the thought.
It is the divine right of cats
To look at kings
And i do not like what i see
Vive la République!
For my part as I scratched at the ice on the car window
I could not believe it
The coffee tasted so good and the bread so solid
The busy hum of the commuter traffic
Seemed to be singing prosperity and security
The rot arrested
By the unexpected chill
The birds shrugged
The wheel turns, they said.

EXPOSURE

Today is milder
Duller and heavier
Get your Alexandrines out
Cackled the gnome Today
Is National Poetry Day The new
Rock and Roll
Pop has been highjacked by the machine.
People have beat a hasty retreat
To the Word
It's time for supermarket poetry
Shrink-wrapped to keep it fresh
Those fragile introspective wanderings
Buffed to solemn religious shine

The cat brushed her whiskers.
If I should die, she said
Think only this of me
Greg was poisoned by a lettuce
You understand
    It's tough
        Being
            A slug.

UNTITLED II

Beware the Portillypolitico beast, my son,
His smile is broad but his eyes are narrow,
His talk is blunt but his teeth are sharp.
Beware the illusion of youth with which he cloaks himself,
For the demons he summons are as old as Methuselah.
The name speaks of travel and worldly ways
But his mind is an island.
There is scorn in his demeanour as he bows to the accolade.
His fingers weave a lure
of adulation and power.
The wolves will not touch him.
By day he woos the lambs,
By night he travels alone through the forest.
His paws leave no trace
In the sparkling snow.

GRUMMAGE

Normington scrimbles
Fest leaves prossell in the rove
A-jitter here
A-jitter there
Gremblayne of nisal smoophs across the wobe
Moondangling to the soup of aeons
Nub tribe dances colfurchionly
Dread bristerly an hobdob risting sun
Crorb
    Haringtar
        Sasoling down
That is the nub of the matter
And don't forget
She cried
Quasselling skimpily among the rings
It's carpark tomorrow
Or is it drabday?

CINDERELLA - NO REGRETS

Broke now
Abandoned by husband
    And in-laws
Shunned by the press
Down to my last credit card.

The prince's shimmering castle
Like his love and gallantry
Proved a mirage
After all
A magical illusion, of course, as
Bright and unreal
As the stroke of midnight.

I've grown quite fond of pumpkin
I've no regrets
I was true to myself
And the counsel of my late
Fairy godmother.
Manners? Hah!
Etiquette was a pushover
I never burped in public
And I never ate the garnish.

BLOODY TOURISTS

We climbed to the Eastgate
Ivy bound the ancient walls
We perched on the ruined parapet
Staring out across the fields
To the forest-masted mountains.

Our mother and our prison falls
Dark
The last of the sun slips beneath the water,
The peaks ablaze and stained in glory.
The desiccated mortar drips from the wall
Like the blood that stained the streets
As wave upon wave of courteous invader
Was repulsed
Then cut to a standstill
Then welcomed. You see these invaders
In everyone's eyes, in their hair.
We are all natives and usurpers here.

Hearing nothing but the quiet late summer rhythm
We leaned and talked.
The machines had fallen silent in the pass
They had finished blasting a tunnel through the rock
I thought a little dust perhaps obscured the stars
No matter - our bridgehead, our freedom, our birth
Was ready
Now the invasions could truly begin.

IT'S NOT YOUR FAULT, T. S. ELIOT

Wrack on the shore,
the
Sand is earthy brown and wet beneath my feet
here the waves roar and funnel over the black rocks
I like the spit of the rain against
the spray of the sea
and the sullen comfort of the metal sky
where the gulls sweep like kings.

UNTITLED III

I wonder how she must have felt,
The first intergalactic space traveller
To pass
Betelgeuse.
Perhaps she thought
She must have reached God
By now.
Then she yelled his name
Through the pregnant blackness

Not even an echo

FOR ADRIAN HENRI

if you weren't you, who would you like to be?

Kate Bush Kirsty MacColl Christy Moore
Van Morrison Tintin Asterix
Gaston LaGaffe Le Chat Achille Talon
Tolkien Mervyn Peake

John Irving Simone de Beauvoir
George Eliot Émile Zola Frédéric Mistral
Serge Gainsbourg Higelin Matisse
Magritte Simon Bolivar Walter Scott

Mandela George Mackay Brown
Cervantes Deborah Harry Wendy Cope
Meryl Streep Roger Martin du Gard
Jules Romains Glenys Kinnock

Roger McGough Brian Patten Mike Starkey
Linton Kwesi Johnson Billy Bragg
Terry Pratchett Douglas Adams
Cleese Jones Palin and Idle

Fry and Laurie Veronique Sanson
Garfield Snoopy The Men They Couldn't Hang
Willa Cather The Horslips The Moomins
P.G. Wodehouse Georges Perec

Mary Robinson Erasmus Gordon Cumming
Steve Death Jim Blyth Jacques Prévert
Tommy Hutchinson Ursula LeGuin Bretecher
The Blues Brothers Rob Roy Aretha
    and
        most of all
          the bloke who wrote "Tonight at Noon" and
            "Adrian Henri's Talking After Christmas
                              Blues"

THE KING OF CARLISLE

I'll let my apple core go brown to Carlisle
Emptiness roars in my head
We're all escaping from the grey
The dust, the cough, the terminally undead.
Some of you have the trappings already:
The Herald, the can of Irn Bru
I have a bath-soaked book of Scottish short stories
Seemingly better thumbed than in reality

We tore past the Northampton commuter
like madmen

Space is at a premium
Muttered the King
How will I get the war chariots
With the scything hubcaps through the porchway?
Remove the hubcaps, replied the Queen
There are too many limbless people here already
Have you ever tried to plough a field with one leg?
I can't do that, said the King, I need them for my wars.
Which you always lose
Exactly - then I need the hubcaps to terrorise the people
Or they would rise up against me
They can't rise at all if they've got no legs
You'll be left with a nation of amputees
A people with nothing below the knees
An economy dying by degrees
Have a beer, my dear, and forget the hubcaps
Oh, alright then.

He won his next war

THE MOTHER OF PARLIAMENTS

Thar's a roight reekin stink down on the farm,
Them pigs done shat in their beds again.
Oi leans on that gate
And watches the farmer.
He ain't got no 'old over them swoine
They's funny animals, them pigs
Rubbing their bottoms in their shit,
'appy as spring lambs.
Then someone walking past
Raises 'is 'ead an' sniffs the air.
"Bloimey O'Roilly," 'e says,
"Smells wurser'n a whore's drawers round 'ere
Wot be goin' on, then?"
Them pigs they stops their playin' an' sniffs too.
Gurt 'eck, they croiy wi' one squeal together.
You're roight - wot a pong.
They looks round - but there's
Always one pig - stupider than the rest.
'E 'asn't noticed they've a' stopped playin' loike
Then 'e realises an' stops too.
But it's too late - 'e's out on is tail
loike as not 'e'll be someone's bacon butty afore long.
Them others - they'll be sorry for a whoile
But soon they'll be playin' loike before.

UNTITLED IV

I could draw myself
seated on the floor, legs half crossed
in contemplation of a man
seated on the floor, legs half crossed
in contemplation of a man
fear of solitude saps me
eaten on the page
quietly pared in a thousand directions
there is a hermit inside me
a small troublesome hermit hopping naked and deranged
like a gadfly in his barrel
the door is bolted fast but he grows thinner
soon he will slide between the hinges
and dance cackling across the floor
knocking ornaments
leaving small dusty footprints in the polish
my family will watch amazed
as I lunge at this nimble side-stepping figure
with the wastepaper basket.

DEATH ON THE BYPASS

When we first awoke
Beneath the mound at Finnan
I thought we were in hell.
I cursed the tortures that had brought me here
As the grinding roar drove through my head.
Then I found I could move my limbs;
I stretched and touched my armour - in the darkness
It glimmered like new
Yet it was light to the touch.
The sword lay by my side, untarnished
Keen as the day it plunged hissing into the smithy water.
I rose and pushed open the door of the tomb;
My comrade followed me.

It did not take us long
To understand the evil
That stalked this land.
We must find peace
The roar must be silenced.

The gods have given us new strength
And new skills.
Our chariot is called Morris Minor.
It cuts down those enemies on wheels
As once we cut down the mighty Roman foot.
The power of the new enemy is its destruction.
The angry flashing lights harry us;
They are legion
But we are immortal.
We will make our place of rest
A place of rest
Again.

ROSSBEIGH

We marched shells scrunching under our feet
Towards the watercolour hills
Deeper than sea blue blue sea to our left
The wind in our faces

DINGLE

It rains like this in Dingle
A thin smur hovers between the brightly painted houses
Or a sudden downpour
Scudding off the streets.
Slow, too, the traffic
A camel train of tourist coaches
picking their way around the hairpins
To deposit their swarming, snapping, mackintoshed loads.
If you tire of your toil in Dingle
Perhaps you can step out on to the quay at lunchtime
And dream the dreams of your forefathers
Through the bottleneck
That funnels the ocean into the bay.

MAJOR'S BRITAIN

She stood down
Eventually
In her place
The acceptable face
Of ordinary aspirations
Fingers
Raised
In apology
He offers
Opprobrium
For petty peccadilloes
Titillating distractions
Sapping the moral strength
Of the nation
A country deserves
The leader it gets
Mr Pusillanimity
Grey-jumpered we
Bury ourselves in a parody of our heritage
Drink our old original ale
And meekly turn for home.

E'ENIN' STANNA

Fury
Blast
Storm
Probe
Misery
Amazing
Sensation
Cheat
Quiz
Doomed
Blunder
buss
Journalism

THE DAY THE MOLES STORMED THE B&Q

Ordinarily Tuesday
Nothing much for staff to do
A few diffident paint fanatics
Floated through the B&Q.
Scroggs the manager puffed his chest
The new display for all to see:
"SELF ADHESIVE WINDOW LEADING
BUY TWO PACKS - GET ONE FREE."
The management trainee checked her name tag
Bustled past the teak-stained doors
Oblivious to the scratching
Of a thousand tiny claws.
But soon the noise grew louder
Behind the walls of tin,
Liberace's golden fingertips
Were smothered in the din.
The door was burst wide open
Behind the mushroom toilet bowls,
A stamping chanting velvet army
Flooded in to seize control.
Their tiny Sten guns blazing,
Red bandannas and Gucci specs,
They trampled on the cornicing
And filled the paint shelves full of lead.
From gimlets through to doorknobs
Furry havoc reigned,
The floor was wet with oozing paint
Few standing shelves remained.
Then as the sirens wailed without
The moles began to halt the fray,
Once the lads in blue arrived
The myopic tide had slipped away.

They found Scroggs stapled to the floor
Amid the debris and the glue,
Our DIY skills were sorely tried
The day they stormed the B&Q.

BALLET OF THE BEIGE MACS

Tum Times tum tum
Cha cha chaps
Seated crossword glum
Ta ta ta
Umber umber um
Berella
Be brief be brief
Case pah pah pah
Stan
Dingroom own Lee
Scored last night (pas de deux – just one)
Tutu be late
Tutu work
Issasin
Pirouette is a wet
Of no consequence
Has been willbe
Squeezed out
Telegraph arf arf
Don't buy that
Itsa dog
We've bought a second home in Wiltshire
Kids at school
Doing fine
Cha cha Charlotte OK?
GreatandSophie?
Broke her ankle
Playing croquet
FT weather today

UNTITLED V

Good evening. Here is the news. Roadworkers today protested at the site of the M25 National Park in Surrey. Plans to dig up a symbolic 25 miles of the motorway and convert it to traditional woodland have been steeped in controversy since they were first announced 6 months ago. A spokesman for the Government, 6 year-old Abigail Hewitt, defended the plans, saying that badgers were more important than cars and that people were polluting the environment too much anyway. The now illegal National Roadusers Federation claimed in a coded call to a local radio station that it had sabotaged the entire Civil Service bicycle fleet. Ms Hewitt dismissed these claims as "silly", announcing that her stabilisers had been checked that morning. Meanwhile, scuffles did not break out at the site as social workers moved in in an attempt to persuade the demonstrators to articulate their aggression. Fifteen were taken away for group therapy and poetry workshops. Prime Minister Kirsty MacColl later visited the site, offering the remaining protesters jobs at the Dagenham Ford Organic Aubergine Farm and a swift half down at the Spliff and Dreadlock.

ARNOLD LANE, ACTUARY

As all readers of *Foresight* (the journal for dynamic thrusting actuaries) know, the members of our profession are far from being the dull-witted, grey-suited number crunchers that popular mythology would have us believe. Some of the world's most exciting people are actuaries. To prove it, your favourite read has compiled a series of profiles of some of the most gobsmackingly cool dudes in the business. Here's a foretaste. Read and enjoy. You know you're wicked.

"ARMADILLOS? I race them. I usually win, you know.
FAVOURITE BOOKS? I bet you think I'm going to say Bruggington's Actuarial Analyses, 1923 edition. Well I am. It's a very interesting book, actually. Or should I say actuarily? Ha ha.
HA HA. ANYTHING ELSE YOU FIND PARTICULARLY INTERESTING? The 8:20 from Purley.
WHAT, ALL OF IT? No, only the front four coaches. I also find interesting the paintwork on my Austin Allegro, John Major and a small split about a centimetre long in my garden hose.
DO YOU HAVE A BUSY SOCIAL LIFE? Of course I do, I'm a very interesting person.
WHERE DO YOU GO? Heaven, The Black Cat, Zizi's.
THOSE ARE NIGHTCLUBS. That's right. We party until dawn. So do the armadillos. Have you ever seen an armadillo rave?
ER, NO."

NOT FADE AWAY

Woke up this morning
Got the end of the world blues
Woke up this morning
Got the end of the world blues
I said I

DOMINUS ILLUMINATIO MEA

1983, you will recall,
Was a fragile summer
Of gentle green beauty
Illusions and security
You remember what it was
To show anger and drink
Pungent draughts
Sinking in the grass
Sedately soporific
Amid the sophisms
Punting plagiarising above all
Drinking we cycled
I find myself among the cobbles
Comprehending little
Analysing less
I wrote and argued and whirled
In my tiny cage
You remember there was love and indirection,
Worldly introspection,
Or was it just the dew in the parks
The marks on the bikes
A wheel wobbling incoherent in the gutter?

UNTITLED VI

Your starter for 10, Mr Goode;
Think of something funny
For a pissy wet dark grey
Friday morning.
Funny?
Here am I
Stuck on the Train From Hell
(or Reading, as it is less affectionately known)
And you want me to be funny.
Only joking, Mr Goode,
You've actually won the Miserable Git of the Year Award.
Well, sod off, then.

UNTITLED VII

Nemesis Jones, Reaper Man
Scratches his nose
It's a kind of can-can
People here just don't understand
I'm not some guy with a hood and a scythe
My name is Jones, I'm an ordinary man.
I work too hard, I get no pay
I'm here for eternity, that's a bloody long day
Death ain't pretty, it's a job like the rest
Makes no odds if you're cursed or you're blest
'T ain't me who decides where your soul's gonna rest
But I can sure as hell give you Purgatory if you wanna be my guest
Said Nemesis Jones, Reaper Man
As he tugged at the straggly beard on his chin
Stubbed out a fag, reached for a tin
Belched contentedly, leaned back with a grin.

If you feel kind of strange as if you're gonna die
See a seedy old man look you straight in the eye
As if he's in a hurry and you're making him stressed
Grateful Dead T-shirt stuck to his chest
Don't push at him rudely or shout, "Outa my way"
Or you might just be the punk that makes his day.

MARTYRS TO THE CAUSE OF ART, NO 27

Whistler's mum
Rubbed her tum,
Said, "Now it's time for tea."
"Oh, come, come, come,"
Replied her son,
"I've painted just your knee."

The portrait done,
She took a bun,
Said, "Let me come and see."
She stood in shock.
"My son's a schlock -
That's Great Aunt Zebedee!"

ROYAL GLOOM

Victoria
Spurned euphoria

SHOCK PRICE RISE FROM ITALIAN RENAISSANCE TRAVEL AGENT

Dante
Upped the ante
For Alicante

BAD MANNERS

"Try to be couther,
Luther,"
The devil said
As he ducked his head;
The inkpot hit the wall instead.

DAY OF THE TRIFFIDS

The wide open road
Went off in my head
I found myself lying
On the estuary bed
The chicken killer's victims
Were trussed in a fridge
I think I'll take a drive
Off Tarrilup Bridge

* *c.f. the Triffids album, Born Sandy Devotional*

UNTITLED VIII

It was Christmas in Olde London,
The smog hung grey and damp,
Monoxide-blackened tinsel
Dangled from the lamps.

Delirious happy shoppers,
Spewing cash and eating tags,
Try to take home Christmas
In a dozen plastic bags.

When you're sleeping in the doorways
Wrapped in rags that stink of piss,
Hope to God it doesn't rain or snow;
Give us a quid and I'll drink to this.

THE REALITY SKIN

When we look back
We all know that it had been happening for years.
Thousands of tiny punctures in the fabric
Until, like drops of water on a window pane,
Two, three, four, then a hundred,
They must inevitably join.

We all have our 'critical mass' stories.
Mine is the 1994 Labour Party Conference
(But that's my nostalgic Untoryism).
The event was swallowed in a vortex
Of Disney characters, sexual innuendo and semantics.
What had changed was not the perennial caricature.
It was the manner in which
Reality sidled apologetically out of the back door
And caught the early tram home.
Perhaps the conference really was presided over by Bambi and Thumper
Supported by a pin-up girl and a Christian in short skirts.
The knowledge grows fainter and dissolves in a media myth.

Today the experts agree with one voice.
They point to the Virtual Reality
As the beginning of our glorious New Fantasy,
Which transcends our territorial existence.
But joy is poisoned
By the infinity of our power.

There may be others like me
Who yearn stupidly for pain and hunger and cold.
I should leave my tank and join them.
Perhaps we can drown in the salty sea –
That is, if we still exist.

MR BENDY SAVES THE CONSERVATIVES

There's a neat little job
Going down in Smith Square.
I'm lacing up my bovver boots,
I'm greasing back my hair.
Nothing menial about this one
Nor is it arty-farty.
It's the post of number one big smelly cheese
Of the LavaTory party.

(Singing) Before the nation's bog brush
Pokes you down the pan,
Ditch the pinstriped public R:
Mr Bendy, he's your man.

Only image counts these days.
To start we'll change your name
To something pleasing to the ear
Without that lingering whiff of shame.
We could hold a referendum,
Let the nation choose,
Something bright and wholesome
Like Rubber, Whips or Noose.

You've missed the point - you've worked so hard
To kill the urge to rule at all -
You've handed out the jar of sweeties,
Leaving farce and music hall.
If he could do it then so can you.
We'll tour the land both near and far
With Bottomley's witty, waggish wisecracks
And Dorrell's wailing slide guitar.

(Singing) We're just a blue rinse flying circus,
We're here to entertain.

You know deep down it's going to work 'cos
Of Mr Bendy's mighty right wing brain.

My friend Arthur, he seh:

"It mek no sense, dese market forces,
Deyse greedy, blind an' tek the lot.
We no give a plague of locusts
De job to weed our garden plot."

Don't listen to that moaning minnie. Here's our manifesto. High time we introduced proportional representation - proportional to the value of the house we own. Thank you, Ma'am:

We sell what's left to sell and more so:
The Army, Navy, Hezza's torso.
No need to educate the poor, so
Save lots of taxes for you and me.

That's me, Mr Bendy. Thank you and good night.

UNTITLED IX

It all started when I won the Garrison Keillor lookalike competition.
Suddenly I was in demand.
I consider myself to be an ordinary sort of chap -
Successful merchant banker,
Six-bedroomed house in Putney,
Beautiful wife - director of personnel at a major securities house -
Great Dane,
E-Type (weekends only; the runaround's a 5-Series).
Then greatness was thrust upon me.
My picture appeared in the "Minnesotan Pig Breeders' Gazette."
Allusions were made about my "virtual reality" in select literary circles.
I received a request to address the bimonthly meeting of the Thurso Cultural Workshop;
I think I saw myself on television
But I wasn't sure.
The pressure on my humdrum existence was too great.
Friends shied from playing me at the squash club,
Pleading they were not worthy.
My wife and I wept softly one night over Chablis and Japanese rice crackers.
She said: "I can no longer meet your needs. You must spread your wings.
You need a girl with flat shoes, a tassled skirt and a large maternal bosom."
I swapped my E-Type for a battered yellow T-registration Volvo,
The Great Dane traded himself in for a shaggy cross between
A Saint Bernard and an Old English Sheepdog.
I pulled on a pair of brown corduroy trousers,
I got a job as GK's stand-in.
I endorse the products he can't be bothered with,
Like hummous and outdoor activity holidays down on the farm.
We sometimes sit around a campfire and swap male-bonding stories.
But I still can't see through those glasses.